TACTICAL GUIDE

TO

PRENUPTIAL
AGREEMENTS

IN ARIZONA

TACTICAL GUIDE

TO

PRENUPTIAL
AGREEMENTS
IN ARIZONA

Scott David Stewart, Esq.

An Imprint of Stewart Law Group

www.ArizonaLawGroup.com

Published in 2018 by Stewart Law Group USA

777 E Thomas Rd Ste 210, Phoenix AZ 85014

Phoenix • Scottsdale • Chandler • Glendale
Mesa • Peoria • Tempe • Gilbert

www.ArizonaLawGroup.com

For information please write the publisher:

Stewart Law Group
777 E Thomas Rd Ste 210
Phoenix AZ 85014

Legal Disclaimer

Contents

Acknowledgements

Many friends supported this project with positive energy, kindly sharing their legal experience and thoughts on best practices. My thanks to retired attorney Robert C. Howard, Jr., for his insight and recommendations. To Laura Valade, J.D., for her diligent research and editing. To every attorney with the firm for their professionalism and dedication to improving the legal profession. Most importantly, to my amazing wife and children. They remind me, each and every day, how truly blessed I am.

I

Introduction to Prenuptial Agreements

T his **Tactical Guide to Prenuptial Agreements in Arizona** is an ideal starting point for anyone getting married and wondering whether a "prenup" might be beneficial. Who really needs one? What is required for validity? How is a legal challenge litigated in court? What should the agreement cover? Find out what the prenup is all about. In the pages that follow, the reader will learn the basics about creating a valid, enforceable prenuptial agreement under Arizona law.

What Is a Prenuptial Agreement?

A prenuptial agreement is a binding contract unique in the law. A very special agreement for two very special people. The word "prenuptial" refers to the premarital status of two individuals preparing to marry each other. A prenuptial agreement is only possible when made between prospective spouses in contemplation of their marriage. Getting married is a material condition!

Prenuptial agreements are effective upon marriage, but not before. What happens when the wedding is postponed after the agreement was signed? The two may want to ratify their agreement in writing to revive it and ensure enforceability. If the wedding is called off permanently, then the prenup is invalidated and unenforceable. See ARS § 25-201(1).

For these reasons, prenuptial contracts are also known as premarital agreements. Similarly, postnuptial agreements (or postmarital contracts) are only made between spouses. A postnuptial agreement may have its origins in a prenup. More about postnuptial agreements, modifications, and revoking a prenup in *Chapter 6*.

Prenuptial agreements are not a modern development. These so-called "marriage contracts" have been around for centuries. Here in the U.S., the prevailing view once held premarital agreements contrary to public policy as anti-marriage. That perspective began to change with the Florida Supreme Court's landmark decision in Mr. and Mrs. Posner's divorce. *Posner v. Posner, 233 So2d 381 (Fla. 1970).*

The *Posner* court held the opposite was true. That antenuptial agreements (or prenups) actually promote the public policy of encouraging marriage. How so? By settling property and alimony issues before the wedding even takes place. Especially where one party is extraordinarily wealthy while the other has very limited financial resources. Without a prenup, a marriage of such economic extremes is far less likely to take place at all.

Although it took another two decades, the *Arizona Uniform Premarital Agreement Act* became law in this state on March 25, 1991. The statute as amended is found in ARS § 25-201, et seq.

Drafting a prenup to withstand legal challenge when it really matters—upon divorce or a spouse's death—is not a do-it-yourself project. In addition to spousal maintenance and property division in the event of divorce, some agreements specify each spouse's household duties and financial obligations, how the children will be raised, and more. See ARS § 25-203. An unenforceable or partially enforceable prenup could cause significant problems for both spouses.

In *Chapter 7*, we explain the attorney's role in drafting, negotiating, and reviewing a proposed premarital agreement for the client.

Understand that Arizona's law is intended to encourage marriage generally; to unify expectations and help the relationship work more smoothly. Given roughly half of all first marriages and more than 60% of all second marriages end in divorce, having a prenuptial agreement can ease the financial complexities of marital dissolution by making divorce proceedings significantly less arduous, both emotionally and financially. The same can be said of prenuptial agreements in probate proceedings following a spouse's death. An overview of what must be included for a prenup to be valid is set forth in *Chapter 4*.

As you will see in *Chapter 2*, prenups are not for everyone. Some people view them as unromantic and pessimistic. Twisting the wedding vow to cherish one another "until death do us part" into a cold-hearted exit plan. Standing alone, that is an emotional argument lacking in reason.

Others view premarital contracts more pragmatically, especially when the marriage introduces children from a previous relationship. The more affluent of the two parties may prefer, very reasonably, the security of a known outcome in the event of death or divorce. To that individual (perhaps a wealthy retiree or business owner), the prenup may be an essential ingredient to a successful marriage.

Regardless, prenuptial agreements must always be voluntary as covered in *Chapter 5*. Look to *Chapter 3* for a discussion about the general terms and conditions found in these agreements.

2
Why Get a Prenuptial Agreement?

There are many reasons why couples should consider whether a prenuptial agreement might benefit them. Even if their final decision is "No, it's not for us," the conversation is well worth having. A prenup addresses numerous aspects of married life. The process of negotiating terms and conditions is beneficial in many ways, too. Mainly because it involves thoughtful, honest communication about a shared future. Open communication is an essential ingredient in the recipe for a successful marriage.

Have the Prenup Conversation

How does having the prenup conversation benefit the parties?

Creating Balance

—By creating opportunity for a balanced understanding of community property law in Arizona.

Engaged couples should understand the impact marriage will have on their property, both with and without a prenuptial agreement. This is important to the marriage, to estate planning and probate, and to divorce or legal separation.

Myths about community property and separate property are quickly dispelled with knowledge. "If I deposit my paychecks in a separate account, are they my separate property?" "Is my pension a separate or community asset?"

Couples do not always realize they are forming a 50/50 partnership in Arizona when they marry and reside here. By default, most earnings and debts incurred during the marriage are community property in nature. The impact of community property law may seem unfair to the higher earning spouse. And the impact of probate law may seem unfair to the economically disadvantaged spouse. A well-drafted prenuptial agreement can help them balance their respective concerns.

Managing Finances

—By initiating the conversation about desired money-habits during marriage.

Dissatisfaction over marital finances can put tremendous stress on a relationship. We know this. Yet couples seldom broach the subject before getting married. One spouse may be a saver, the other a spendthrift. Or perhaps both are spendthrifts, prone to quickly get into debt. Even when both are savers, one may not save enough in the opinion of the other.

Preparing a prenuptial agreement necessarily triggers discussions about managing marital finances. Each individual needs to know what he or she is getting into with the other's money habits. Then they can decide how, as a couple, they might adjust their behaviors to be more compatible.

Combining Relations

—By helping blend their families both financially and emotionally.

Seldom is avoiding conflict easy when there is tension between a new spouse and the other party's children from a previous marriage or relationship.

Whether the children are minors or adults, a prenuptial agreement may be instructive following a spouse's death. Responding emotionally, relationships can sour quickly when decedent's children oppose the surviving spouse in probate. Terms agreed to in the prenup can clarify what the surviving spouse is entitled to receive, avoiding a costly, contested probate action.

Understanding Property

—By delving into the legal concepts of transmutation and commingling.

That is, by understanding what actions transform one spouse's separate assets into community property owned by both of the spouses.

The spouse who brings substantial wealth to the marriage may be concerned about preserving that wealth. Say, for example, to benefit his or her children from a previous marriage.

Maintaining Control

—By providing agreement and flexibility in handling marital assets and debts during the marriage.

Rather than requiring spouses follow Arizona's community property system, the prenuptial agreement puts them in control of how their assets and liabilities will be shared. This also gives them greater flexibility in how they will provide for one another. For instance, the amount and duration of spousal maintenance may be agreed upon in the event there is a divorce.

Dignifying Death

—By initiating important end of life conversations.

Some discussions are difficult. As are discussing healthcare, chronic medical conditions, passing of a spouse, long-term care needs, and desired end-of-life care. These are discussions all couples who plan to marry should have, regardless of age. For a mature individual planning a second marriage, statistically the number of years ahead are fewer than the years passed. A prenuptial agreement may include provisions intended to mesh with each spouse's estate plan.

Dignifying Divorce

—By allowing the spouses to terminate their marriage with dignity while protecting their private lives from courtroom discovery.

If parties have a prenuptial agreement and choose to divorce, then they need not wallow in the muck, air their dirty laundry, or otherwise expose their personal lives and unhappy relationship in court. Instead, they point to the terms of their prenup which serves as the guiding instrument in their break-up.

Saving Resources

—By saving money through orderly disposition of property in the event of a spouse's death or upon the couples' divorce.

The cost of hiring attorneys to prepare the prenuptial agreement is typically less, often substantially less, than incurring the expense of litigating a divorce or contested probate action. Should the relationship fall apart, the prenup can save on time and litigation costs by providing for a clear, orderly disposition of accumulated wealth and liabilities.

In the absence of a prenup, Arizona's divorce statutes and case law will only provide general guidelines. This makes specific results at trial unpredictable. Uncertainty of outcome is an important factor in leading people to risk litigation over settlement. However, litigation always comes with significant cost.

Although rare, it is possible for parties to execute a premarital agreement and have the marriage annulled.

There are many grounds for annulment of marriage in ARS § 25-301: Fraud, bigamy, lack of parental consent to a son's or daughter's underage marriage, mental illness, duress, and so on. What happens to a prenup when the marriage is annulled? With a void marriage, one that has been annulled, the court will only consider enforcing those terms of the agreement that must be upheld in order to avoid inequitable results. See also ARS § 25-202(F).

Do the points listed above mirror your concerns or pique an interest in the potential benefits of negotiating a married future? Keep reading. The next step is to determine how you and your intended might benefit from a personalized premarital contract.

Who Needs a Prenup?

A prenuptial agreement is an action plan of the parties own making. The agreement includes terms and conditions effective upon the passing of specified events. For instance, an agreed term may provide the economically dependent spouse a predetermined amount of spousal maintenance if they legally separate or divorce. An agreed condition may be that the planned purchase of a vacation home can only follow a debt free marital residence. The agreement could expressly state each spouse's portion of the mortgage payment.

What's the takeaway? Having flexibility and control over what happens with the marriage down the road. Ten years or so in the future (with married life no longer hypothetical) the spouses could choose to modify their prenup, revoke it in its entirety, create a superseding postmarital contract, or do nothing more at all.

Considerations Worthy of Negotiation

To retain flexibility and control tomorrow, give marriage careful consideration today. Marriage is one huge commitment. Planning an idyllic wedding is exciting, a lifetime experience that should be joyful and memorable. But negotiating terms and conditions for a prenuptial agreement means imagining what this marriage could be and should be. That is not a simple task. (Especially if a first marriage for both—uncharted territory.) Start the conversation by raising the following key questions.

Assets and Debts

Is a prenup necessary to protect significant assets? Is there a substantial imbalance of wealth or income? Are circumstances such that one will bring substantial debt to the marriage? What percentage of income will each spouse apply to funding an IRA, 401k, or other retirement plan?

Involving a certified financial advisor or Certified Public Accountant (CPA) may be necessary as well for fruitful negotiations between the parties with their lawyers' assistance.

Children

Is this a second marriage for either party? Does either have children from a previous marriage or relationship? What is the plan for raising a child? Creating a plan for the child's treatment—during the marriage, with divorce, upon a parent's death—will take careful consideration. Be sure to build flexibility and control into the prenup.

Professional Practices or Business Interests

Is either party a business owner? In the absence of a prenuptial agreement, a business with a community interest is divided upon dissolution of marriage or upon the death of the spouse who was the primary operator. This could mean termination of the organization and the end of a steady income stream. Consider, too, the consequences of dividing a professional practice as a marital asset in divorce.

Retirement Ages

What about age? Is one party significantly older than the other? On the wedding day, the younger spouse may have many earning-years ahead while the older spouse is already drawing a pension or approaching retirement on a fixed income.

Lovers may not care much about age differences, but age disparity may be cause for financial concern. If divorce results in an equal, or nearly equal, division of community assets and debts, then the financial resources of the older spouse may never be sufficiently recovered to provide for his or her own retirement.

In Arizona property division law, each spouse owns one-half of the community estate (assets and debts). Could that division be altered? Yes! By separation agreement negotiated during the divorce and by prenuptial agreement executed before the marriage.

A valid prenup may include a property division plan that not only deviates from the 50/50 presumed division under Arizona law, but which also plans for the late-in-life needs of the elder spouse.

College and Professional Degrees

Might one spouse willingly support the other so their marriage benefits from future income generated through the other spouse's college or professional degree?

One spouse may work two or three jobs to cover household and tuition expenses. Doing so allows the other spouse to concentrate on coursework and focus on obtaining the degree that will, they believe, ultimately benefit the marital community. Sometimes spouses postpone having children as well.

What is a fair division of property if this couple gets divorced or separates? Or upon death, how should the decedent's estate be shared? What if survivors include decedent's children from a previous marriage? Again, a prenup is about control with flexibility.

Inheritances and Gifts

Does either spouse anticipate receiving a substantial inheritance during the marriage? A provision in the prenuptial agreement could determine how inheritance is handled upon a spouse's death. The prenup could provide that any inheritance remains the beneficiary's separate property despite his or her actions during the marriage. Actions that, in the absence of a prenup, would be commingling, transmutation, or gift to the community under Arizona law.

With an experienced family law attorney's help during negotiations, drafting, and execution, a prenuptial agreement can resolve these and other complex issues. The attorney knows that, when the time arrives to enforce the agreement, the court must determine whether all of the substantive terms are fair. And whether procedural fairness existed in negotiating and executing the agreement before the wedding.

3

Terms and Conditions in Prenuptial Agreements

A prenuptial agreement does much in the way of planning ahead for a compatible and companionable married life. But some things are strictly off limits. Couples cannot agree to an act that violates public policy. Nor can they contract to do something criminal or illegal. For example, an "agreement" to commit tax evasion by hiding earnings from the IRS could never be enforced in court by one spouse against the other.

Arizona's statute lists the scope of what is permissible with a prenuptial agreement and what is expressly prohibited. The language of ARS § 25-203 is broad, allowing parties to negotiate reasonable terms with substantial flexibility:

A. Parties to a premarital agreement may contract with respect to:

1. The rights and obligations of each of the parties in any of the property of either or both of them whenever and wherever acquired or located.

2. The right to buy, sell, use, transfer, exchange, abandon, lease, consume, expend, assign or create a security interest in, mortgage, encumber, dispose of or otherwise manage and control property.

3. The disposition of property on separation, marital dissolution, death or the occurrence or nonoccurrence of any other event.

4. The modification or elimination of spousal support.

5. The making of a will, trust or other arrangement to carry out the provisions of the agreement.

6. The ownership rights in and disposition of the death benefit from a life insurance policy.

7. The choice of law governing the construction of the agreement.

8. Any other matter, including their personal rights and obligations, not in violation of public policy or a statute imposing a criminal penalty.

B. The right of a child to support may not be adversely affected by a premarital agreement.

Now take a look at terms and conditions typically found in Arizona prenuptial agreements.

Providing for Spousal Maintenance

First on the list of terms and conditions is spousal maintenance in the event of divorce or legal separation. (Known as alimony in some jurisdictions.) Most challenges to prenuptial agreements involve spousal support, usually because the couple accumulated more during the marriage and the prenup does not account for those assets. Talk to a lawyer.

Arizona law allows for agreements to modify or eliminate support of a spouse. These are often fixed in a prenup. An individual may waive the right to financial support if upon separation or divorce in the future. *Note: Either or both spouses may waive the right to spousal maintenance.*

There is an exception regarding waivers, however. The prenup cannot eliminate support or curtail payments to the point where the now economically dependent spouse is impoverished as a consequence.

ARS § 25-202(D) states as follows:

> "If a provision of a premarital agreement modifies or eliminates spousal support and that modification or elimination causes one party to the agreement to be eligible for support under a program of public assistance at the time of separation or marital dissolution, a court, notwithstanding the terms of the agreement, may require the other party to provide support to the extent necessary to avoid that eligibility."

In other words, such a detrimental provision or waiver would be unenforceable. Here's a quick test of whether the party's waiver of the right to support will ultimately be unenforceable: Will the waiving party become eligible for public assistance (welfare) for lack of support by the other spouse? If "Yes," then the support waiver cannot be wholly enforced.

Providing for Property Succession

Second on the list of prenup terms and conditions regards property—separate and community. Treatment of assets and debts during marriage makes up the most widely used provisions. For purposes of Arizona prenuptial agreements, "property" includes income, earnings, and any "interest, present or future, legal or equitable, vested or contingent" in the parties' real property (including interests in real estate) or personal property. ARS § 25-201(2).

Not only are couples free to determine how property will be bought, sold, used, transferred, mortgaged, and managed during the marriage, but they may also decide how property will be divided in the event of divorce or legal separation. Before they marry, couples are free to negotiate division of community property, valuation of assets, allocation of debts, and the like.

Lots of important decisions may be made before the wedding. Who will keep the house? How will the mortgage be paid? Who gets which investment fund? Who shall have controlling interest of the family business? Both spouses work from the same game plan on marriage, separation, divorce, and untimely death of a spouse. Similar to a separation agreement settling property division in divorce, they may characterize future assets and debts as either separate or community property. Pretty amazing, really.

Consider other assets, such as pensions and retirement accounts. Absent prenup to the contrary, in Arizona divorce law a pension or retirement account wholly funded during the marriage fits neatly within the legal definition of community property. ARS § 25-211. And in divorce, community property is divided equally between the spouses. By prenuptial agreement, either individual may waive his or her future marital interest in the other's IRA, pension, or 401k funded with marital earnings. If the right to a community share of the other spouse's retirement asset was waived by the prenup, then upon death or divorce the retirement asset is, by agreement, not marital property.

Attorney Fees and Costs

The parties to a prenuptial agreement can also negotiate who shall pay the cost of preparing the prenup. This is particularly helpful when a wealthy individual wants a prenup in order to get married, but the other party needs financial assistance in order to hire his or her own attorney. As discussed later, having one's own attorney to assist in negotiating and drafting the prenuptial agreement is paramount. If the financially dominant party wholly controls the negotiation and the other party cannot afford to obtain review by independent counsel, then enforcement becomes problematical. What's the point of an invalid or unenforceable prenup? Get it right from the get go.

The agreement may also provide for the payment of legal fees, court costs, forensic valuations, child custody evaluations, and related expenses in divorce or legal separation proceedings. Additionally, the couple can agree on how probate court costs and expenses related to administration of the decedent's estate will be paid.

Will the costs be paid from community resources, for instance, or from the deceased spouse's separate bank or investment account?

Taxation Matters

A prenuptial agreement may include provisions addressing tax matters. The parties could designate responsibility for preparing a joint tax return, especially if one is more sophisticated or has specialized expertise or training in that area. They may agree upon the portion each will contribute to the payment of taxes if, for example, one's income is substantially greater than the other's. Couples might agree that each will be responsible for taxes owed on separate property income and will pay the tax owed from a separate bank account. While agreeing to keep income earned on separate property segregated for tax purposes, too.

Deciding how tax matters will be handled in marriage is reason to consult a CPA or tax attorney. Before accepting any arrangement, understand current law and how the proposed prenup agreement alters the outcome. Consider a recent example.

Along with other sweeping changes to U.S. tax law, the so-called "alimony deduction" was effectively repealed in 2019 by the *Tax Cuts and Jobs Act of 2017, Public Law No. 115-97*. (TCJA sunsets after 2025.)

Prior tax law allowed the payor to deduct spousal maintenance payments from income on his or her individual income tax return, an above-the-line deduction taken without itemization. (See IRS Publication 504.) Under prior law, it was the payee as recipient who included payments as income. The TCJA eliminated the alimony deduction, effectively doing away with the requirement a recipient include spousal support as income.

That is still how it works after 2018 for taxpayers grandfathered under prior law allowing the deduction. The date of the order or decree determines whether the payor is grandfathered under prior law allowing a deduction for alimony payments. The separation instrument's date must be no later than December 31, 2018, for taxpayers to claim the alimony deduction.

Now consider how spousal maintenance is negotiated in divorce or legal separation. Typically, the wealthier party is asked to support the economically dependent spouse, at least for a time. How much and for how long? Amount and duration depend upon financial need, ability to pay, and many other spousal maintenance factors. See ARS § 25-319.

Among the two, the payor is likely to be in the higher income tax bracket. The alimony deduction represented a tax break for the payor. The recipient included alimony as income and was assessed the tax, but at a lower tax rate, perhaps much lower. During negotiations, the deduction incentivized paying more to support a dependent spouse who, in turn, enjoyed a lower tax rate (an incentive to seek higher support). A win-win situation. But things changed on January 1, 2019. For separation instruments entered after 2018, the alimony deduction is unavailable.

Although there is no alimony deduction under TCJA rules, there is a special rule for post-decree modifications. In modifying spousal maintenance ordered before 2019, the parties have a choice:

A) When better served by TCJA rules (no alimony deduction), they can expressly provide that the TCJA rules shall apply to their spousal maintenance modification; or

B) When better served by pre-TCJA rules, they can maintain grandfathered status under prior law on their modified pre-2019 divorce decree (alimony deduction allowed).

A prenup may be used to obtain a more beneficial arrangement than TCJA or other law would otherwise dictate in absence of agreement. Be mindful that laws and rules on these and other family concerns could change anytime. Prepare to discuss various outcomes under current law with an attorney.

On the Child's Upbringing

Some couples include terms and conditions in a premarital agreement that attempt to control custody upon a parent's death or divorce. Child custody is a general term meant to include both legal decision-making authority and parenting time access to the child. Custody terms are not something that can be constrained via prenup, though.

Why is that? A premarital agreement cannot limit a party's constitutionally protected parental rights. The right to parent one's child is within the due process clauses of the Fifth and Fourteenth Amendments to the U.S. Constitution. Nor can the prenup provide a parenting plan that is not in the child's best interests.

Arizona custody law takes precedence over a premarital agreement with child custody terms. Couples cannot use a prenup to dictate parenting time or who shall have legal decision-making over a child if they separate or divorce. That is for the court to determine based upon statutory factors weighed according to what is in the child's best interests. (See ARS § 25-403.)

Furthermore, a prenup cannot attempt to divest the court of custody jurisdiction over a minor child. If divorce with children happens, then parents should negotiate a parenting plan in good faith with their attorneys' assistance and submit their parenting plan to the court.

Having said that, a couple might want to provide personal guidance for married life by reciting intentions regarding custody. For example, by stating their mutual desire for joint custody and equal parenting time if they divorce. They might agree to one parent being the primary caregiver who works from home until the child reaches a certain age. What if that parent chooses a different career path? That is his or her personal right. Could the other spouse sue to enforce a prenup that requires the other parent work from home or not at all? Of course not.

Understand how some wishes affect personal rights and obligations and, as such, are not enforceable and will not bind the judge in divorce proceedings. In any case, such a provision should be made severable from the premarital contract without affecting the overall validity and enforceability of the agreement's remaining terms and conditions.

Provisions directing the child's upbringing and education may be included in a prenup, although court enforcement might not always be forthcoming. Compare a proviso over education with a proviso over religious upbringing. An agreement the child shall attend private school and receive private lessons in music and the arts may be enforceable in divorce proceedings. By contrast, an agreement on the child's religious upbringing may not be enforceable. Courts generally do not interfere with a parent's decision to expose the child to a religious practice or belief that, standing alone, violates the prenuptial contract's religious-upbringing term. The exception being evidence of substantial risk of actual harm to the child from the religious practice or belief.

Additional Child Support

Can a couple provide for child support obligations and amounts in their premarital agreement? In Arizona law, a prenup cannot adversely impact child support. For instance, the agreement cannot determine which parent will be wholly responsible for paying child support. Parties can agree on extra support for such things as private lessons, extracurricular activities, travel, and so on.

With every custody proceeding, the court will order child support based upon calculations using the *Arizona Child Support Guidelines*. No child should be made to suffer for lack of support simply because his or her parents entered into a premarital contract with terms contrary to the Guidelines.

Future parents can agree to child support in excess of what the Guidelines require, but cannot reduce or eliminate child support in violation of the Guidelines. For example, they could agree to the wealthier parent providing additional monthly support, paying child-related expenses for extracurricular activities, and funding a college trust. But couples cannot agree to eliminate or diminish a parent's legal obligation to support their child.

Generally, a prenuptial agreement cannot negatively impact the rights of third parties to the agreement, such as the creditor of one or both spouses. A provision in the agreement that creates a beneficial right in a child may be enforced by that child as a third party beneficiary. Say the prenup included a provision to fund a college trust, as an example, but the parents either failed to pay into the trust or removed funds from the educational trust for some other purpose.

Consult an attorney about the scope of third-party rights created by prenuptial contract.

4

What Is Required for Validity?

Validity of a premarital agreement must be proven in court if relevant to the outcome of a contested probate proceeding or divorce. A contest can occur when one party desires spousal maintenance in the divorce, for example, and challenges the prenup provision eliminating the other spouse's obligation to pay such spousal support.

The best assurance the court will uphold the terms of a prenup is to "dot the i's and cross the t's"—make sure every procedural and substantive step in the process is conducted properly and lawfully. First of all, a prenup must be in writing and signed by the party to be charged. Meaning it must be signed by the spouse against whom enforcement is sought.

For the parties' agreement to withstand challenge by an adverse party in a divorce or probate action, it must be valid. To be valid, a prenup must satisfy all requirements in ARS § 25-202:

> A. A premarital agreement must be in writing and signed by both parties. The agreement is enforceable without consideration.
>
> B. The agreement becomes effective on marriage of the parties.
>
> C. The agreement is not enforceable if the person against whom enforcement is sought proves either of the following:
>
> 1. The person did not execute the agreement voluntarily.
>
> 2. The agreement was unconscionable when it was executed and before execution of the agreement that person:
>
> (a) Was not provided a fair and reasonable disclosure

of the property or financial obligations of the other party.

(b) Did not voluntarily and expressly waive, in writing, any right to disclosure of the property or financial obligations of the other party beyond the disclosure provided.

(c) Did not have, or reasonably could not have had, an adequate knowledge of the property or financial obligations of the other party.

D. If a provision of a premarital agreement modifies or eliminates spousal support and that modification or elimination causes one party to the agreement to be eligible for support under a program of public assistance at the time of separation or marital dissolution, a court, notwithstanding the terms of the agreement, may require the other party to provide support to the extent necessary to avoid that eligibility.

E. An issue of unconscionability of a premarital agreement shall be decided by the court as a matter of law.

F. If a marriage is determined to be void, an agreement that would otherwise have been a premarital agreement is enforceable only to the extent necessary to avoid an inequitable result.

As discussed previously, prenuptial agreements are a unique type of contract. One special characteristic is that consideration per se (something of value given in exchange for a promise) is not required to bind the parties to "the deal." A binding agreement allows the court to enforce it against the violating party. Still, many argue that the promise to marry is adequate consideration when in exchange for a promise to sign a premarital agreement. With the requirement of consideration satisfied, the remaining requirements for validity are legal capacity to contract and voluntariness.

Legal Capacity to Contract

Does the person have the requisite legal capacity to enter into a prenuptial agreement? If the prenup is challenged in the parties' divorce, for instance, then the court will look back to the circumstances surrounding the execution of the agreement.

A party to a contract must have the ability to understand the nature, extent, character, and effect of the contract. He or she must be able to reasonably understand what signing the agreement will do in terms of limiting or waiving marital rights. Ability to understand the contract and an actual understanding of the contract are two distinct concepts, though.

Contracting Must Have Been Voluntary

A contract must be voluntary. Prenuptial agreements are, by their very nature, prone to being executed under emotional circumstances. For some, the marriage may not happen at all if the prenuptial agreement goes unsigned. Therefore, the courts look more closely at the requirement that it be a voluntarily entered agreement and not something else. The requirement of voluntariness cannot be waived by either party.

Voluntariness means the signing was intentional and not coerced. What does involuntariness look like? An agreement was entered into involuntarily if the individual was coerced into signing it. Coercion may be through fraud, duress, undue influence, or overreaching. The individual under duress is coerced into signing the contract by another's unlawful threat. Because of that threat, the weaker party had no alternative but to sign the agreement.

When undue influence destroys voluntariness, the individual was deprived of any meaningful choice. His or her freedom of choice to decide whether to execute the agreement or not was effectively substituted by the will of another (usually the other party to the prenuptial agreement, but not always). For instance, the parties' relationship may involve a weaker individual who is emotionally and financially controlled by a dominant partner. Or an overbearing parent who desires the prenup could unduly influence a son or daughter into executing the agreement. Undue influence is always something to look for among those in a close relationship, such as family, friends, coworkers, and two people planning to spend married life together.

With premarital agreements, contract validity also demands fairness, both procedurally and substantively. To satisfy procedural fairness, voluntariness is essential. With substantive fairness, if the agreement was unconscionable when signed, then it should be held invalid. See ARS § 25-202(C)(1,2).

What does unconscionability mean in this context? An unconscionable agreement is one that shocks the conscience or is expressly unconscionable according to statute. The judge determines unconscionability as a question of law. See ARS § 25-202(E).

A valid prenup is supported by fair and reasonable disclosure of the property or financial obligations of both individuals. Substantive unfairness may result if there was inadequate or nonexistent financial disclosure of assets and debts.

The most common situation of substantive unfairness involves a party who did not know, and could not have known, about the other's finances. Without proper disclosure, the agreement is unconscionable having lacked substantive fairness ab initio, or from the beginning. Unlike voluntariness, however, a party can waive the right to fair and reasonable financial disclosure. *Repeat: A party can waive his or her right to full financial disclosure.* More on that next.

5

Proving Voluntariness in the Courtroom

Familiar with the adage, "It's not a problem until it's a problem"? With most spouses, the prenuptial agreement does not undergo judicial scrutiny for years, perhaps decades, after its execution. The problem spouses encounter is discovering potential vulnerabilities with the agreement when enforcement is sought by one or both parties. As with any contract, the ideal time to make corrections and adjustments is after review by independent counsel and before signing it. However, that is not how things always play out.

Problems with the premarital agreement surface quickly when one party asks the court to enforce it while the other party objects on one or more grounds. A challenge initiates multi-factor analysis by the court. Something a bit more in-depth than establishing "Who drafted it?"

Statute of Limitations

Enforcement of the prenuptial agreement in probate or family court often occurs many years after the instrument was signed. By contrast, with a breach of contract or personal injury lawsuit, the years gone by without the plaintiff taking any legal action would result in dismissal. Why? Because the complaint was filed too late, outside the statute of limitations period.

With enforcement of a premarital agreement, though, marriage tolls the clock allowing a spouse to sue and enforce the prenup decades after the agreement was signed. A special limitations period for prenups is set forth in ARS § 25-205:

> "A statute of limitations applicable to an action asserting a claim for relief under a premarital agreement is tolled during the marriage of the parties to the agreement. However, equitable defenses limiting the time for enforcement, including laches and estoppel, are available to either party."

Consequently, arguments that prenup enforcement should be time-barred are only available in equity. Those equitable defenses include: Laches because of the spouse's unreasonable delay in seeking prenup enforcement; estoppel given the spouse's previous conduct; and the spouse's unclean hands for having acted in bad faith, among others.

Who Carries the Burden of Proof in Court?

When a premarital agreement's validity is challenged in a divorce or probate action, responsibility for carrying the burden of proof is an essential aspect of the case.

At the trial or hearing, the court opens with the legal presumption the spouses' premarital agreement is valid. From there, the opponent of the prenup (the spouse challenging validity) carries the initial burden of proof and must make a prima facie case of the agreement's invalidity. The burden of proof then shifts to the proponent of the premarital agreement—he or she must offer evidence of the prenup's validity. (See *Pownall v. Pownall* below.) The judge begins the analysis with several important voluntariness factors. Will the agreement withstand judicial scrutiny?

Voluntariness Factors

With divorce or probate pending, validity of the premarital agreement may be challenged by either spouse (or both), by the deceased spouse's executor, or by a third-party beneficiary of the contract. A prenup could be set aside for a number of reasons.

What factors should the court consider when determining whether the agreement was voluntarily entered into? The parties introduce relevant evidence of the following:

1. Competency

Did the party have legal capacity to contract at the time he or she signed the agreement? Was he or she mentally incompetent at the time? Did the spouse sign the prenuptial agreement under the influence of drugs or alcohol?

2. Financial Disclosure

Was there any fraud to induce the party into signing the prenuptial agreement? Did a party materially misrepresent his or her property and debts? Misrepresentation occurs when a party misleads or hides assets or liabilities from the other party.

Parties to a prenup may include a recital, or statement, about how they know everything they need to know and how they made financial disclosures before executing the contract. Full financial disclosure of assets and debts is very important, but the right to fair and reasonable disclosure of property and financial obligations may be waived. (An experienced family lawyer would likely advise against such waiver). Not surprisingly, the waiver must be voluntary, express, and in writing.

There are various ways to make sufficient financial disclosures: Itemized statements; statements of net worth and income (summary); provision of financial records with raw data; verbal exchange of financial information; business profit and loss statement; and informal disclosure providing "constructive knowledge" of the offering spouse's financial picture.

Constructive knowledge is based upon pre-existing, informally-obtained financial information. Knowledge is gathered by observation and communications occurring before and during the couple's courtship. Setting romance aside for just a moment, relying on the outward appearance of someone's lifestyle without concrete evidence of net worth and income is, well, a dicey proposition. Avoid it.

A person may enjoy an high standard of living, but be massively in debt. Hence the need for full disclosure of property and finances. Worse, a carefully planned facade of wealth could rise to the level of intentional fraud. Purposefully inducing a paramour into marriage by rubbing elbows with all the right people and appearing at exclusive social occasions. Someone who appears to be of modest means may, in fact, be quite wealthy. Howard Hughes—among the most financially successful people in the world—was said to dress like a bum. Looks can be deceiving and often are.

3. Independent Legal Advice

Each spouse should have an attorney participate in drawing up the premarital agreement. Although having one's own attorney is not essential to a prenuptial contract's validity, obtaining independent legal counsel is a very strong indicator of voluntariness. Actually, it is probably the single most important factor supporting voluntariness when the agreement is challenged in court by a party.

What if the attorney's recommendation was "don't sign the prenup as written," but the client signed it anyway? The attorney's recommendation was still independent legal advice despite the client's rejection.

What if the drafting party recommended the other party obtain independent legal advice before deciding whether or not to sign the agreement, but the other party rejected that recommendation and signed without an attorney's review? Knowing and having opportunity to obtain independent legal advice is still evidence of voluntariness. See *Pownall v. Pownall, 197 Ariz. 577, 5 P3d 911 (Ariz. Ct. App. 2000).*

4. Timing

When the prenuptial agreement was presented for execution is yet another important factor when considering voluntariness. Generally, premarital agreements should be finalized at least one month before the wedding ceremony.

Did the drafting party spring the prenup on the other spouse an hour before the wedding? 24 hours before? A week before? Springing a prenuptial agreement on the other party the day before the wedding is no way to start a marriage. Doing so is a sure way to have the prenup set aside by the court for lack of voluntariness, too.

Instead, plan to allow sufficient time for reasonable reflection. What is considered a reasonable period for reflection will depend upon the circumstances and, also, whether the whole matter of a premarital agreement was raised, discussed, and arranged before presentment for execution.

5. Knowledge of Marital Rights

This voluntariness factor ties in with the importance of obtaining independent legal advice and having actual knowledge of the other party's financial affairs. First, each party should know what his or her marital rights and obligations will be under the law. Second, each should know how the premarital agreement will impact those marital rights. Namely, those are community property rights and interests along with spousal maintenance rights and obligations in Arizona law.

Understand, as well, that a waiver of those marital rights must be made voluntarily and intelligently for it to be enforced against the waiving spouse.

There are limits on what a party can waive. Before signing any agreement, discuss marital rights and obligations with an attorney along with the potential consequences of waiving those rights.

6. Overreach, Duress, Undue Influence

Whether there was overreaching, duress, or undue influence depends upon the circumstances and is not always obvious. Consider the voluntariness of the following circumstances:

Threats

Were there threats? Duress includes a threat of violence, which would be persuasive evidence of involuntariness. By contrast, threatening not to marry unless the prenup is signed is not persuasive evidence of duress.

Pregnancy

Nor is it persuasive for the woman to be so worried about being pregnant that she signed the prenup papers.

Language Fluency

With a potential language barrier, as with an immigrant who is not fluent in English (or not fluent in the same language as the other party), the requisite level of communication in English sufficient to support validity is *low*.

Emotionally Resistant

It is not enough for a spouse to testify at trial: "I didn't want to sign the agreement." A party's emotional opposition to signing the prenuptial agreement, but who signed off anyway, is not considered persuasive evidence of involuntariness.

Unequal Bargaining Power

This, too, is not persuasive because prenups almost always involve an imbalance of bargaining power. Negotiating a fair deal is a key reason for why both individual's should obtain independent legal advice.

Oral Promises

Verbal agreements that were never written into the premarital agreement are not persuasive evidence of involuntariness. However, on the issue of whether a party's waiver was voluntary, it may be useful to show the parties discussed the prenup and possible terms well in advance of the written instrument's presentation for the party's execution.

Deliberate Ignorance

What if a party was properly presented with the agreement, but opted not to read it? Choosing not to read the premarital agreement before signing it is a personal choice. However, failure to read the instrument and choosing to blindly sign it is not persuasive evidence of an involuntary agreement.

Love

Does love change everything? Say, for instance, the party who wanted a premarital agreement made extraordinarily generous provisions for the other party. But in their divorce, that same spouse argued the prenup should be set aside for undue influence because he was blinded by love. As one might expect, being blinded by love is not persuasive evidence of involuntariness.

6

Amendments, Revocations & Postmarital Agreements

Previously, we emphasized the flexibility and control that a well-drafted, thoughtfully-negotiated prenuptial agreement can provide. Still, the spouses may wish to make changes to their contract after they have been married for a while. In fact, they may choose to revoke the agreement altogether.

Can a premarital agreement be changed or terminated after the marriage? Yes, so long as all legal formalities are adhered to. Spouses may revoke their agreement. Doing so restores their marital rights under the law and puts them back in the position they would have been in had there been no prenuptial agreement at all.

Just as the prenuptial agreement must be in writing, any modification or revocation of the prenup must also be made in writing and must be signed by both spouses. No matter how many times the conversation surfaced over the years, verbalizing a mutual desire to cancel the contract does not make it so.

Mutual countervailing actions are also insufficient to revoke a prenup. For example, the spouses' decision to use separate funds to satisfy the mortgage on their marital home does not, in and of itself, terminate the prenuptial agreement. Even if it provides that separate property shall never be used to pay a community debt. As a rule, neither oral modifications nor oral revocations are valid.

Arizona's ARS § 25-204 controls amendments and revocations of prenuptial agreements:

> After marriage, a premarital agreement may be amended or revoked only by a written agreement signed by the parties. The amended agreement or the revocation is enforceable without consideration.

Spouses who have been married for years might want to amend, revoke, or replace their old contract with a fresh agreement. For example, if the economically dependent spouse will not get a fair benefit upon divorce or probate and this is causing strife, then the parties may want to amend their prenup. The law controlling prenuptial agreements is statutory. Amending a prenuptial agreement after the marriage does not transform it into a postnuptial contract. Those are two distinct instruments controlled by two distinct bodies of law.

Assuming no divorce or legal separation is pending in court, the spouses could choose to substitute their premarital agreement entirely with a postmarital contract. Particularly if doing so promotes marital harmony. Couples who never had a prenup may want to talk to a family law attorney about a postnuptial contract.

Postmarital Agreements in Arizona

In Arizona, spouses may enter into postmarital agreements that cover similar territory as premarital agreements: Categorizing and dividing property, providing spousal maintenance, funding a child's college trust, and so on.

This may be surprising, but there was a time in Arizona when a wife could not enter into a contract with her husband. An important case by the name of *In re Estate of Harber, 104 Ariz. 79, 449 P2d 7 (1969)*, did away with that antiquated notion.

In 1969, the Arizona Supreme Court in Harbor's Estate enforced a postmarital contract that provided for the wife upon her husband's death. Given the close relationship between the parties, to be valid and enforceable a postmarital agreement must be fair and equitable, be entered into with full knowledge of the property, and be free from fraud, coercion, and undue influence. The proponent of the postmarital contract has the burden of proving in court, by clear and convincing evidence, that the agreement was properly executed.

More recently, the Arizona Court of Appeals held that sophisticated LLC operating agreements which placed "permanent and significant limitations" on a spouse's property rights and which transferred substantial control to the other spouse were, therefore, "no less severe than a more traditional postnuptial property division agreement." *Austin v. Austin, No. 2 CA-CV 2014-0134 (Ariz. Ct. App. April 30, 2015)*.

The appeals court in *Austin* held that the requirements of *Harber's Estate* applied to the operating agreements because:

> "[T]he mere use of a limited liability company to effectuate changes to the property rights of spouses does not transmute such an agreement into an arm's-

length business transaction... Because the operating agreements were made during [the] marriage and altered each spouse's property rights in the event of death, the [llc] operating agreements meet the definition of postnuptial agreement. Therefore, the requirements of Harber's Estate apply."

In short, the duck test applies.

Needless to say, creating a postmarital agreement is a whole new ball game. Again, sound legal advice is essential for the best possible outcome. Be mindful that the law of postnuptial contracts is not the same as that of prenuptial agreements. (Postmarital agreements are governed by caselaw, not statutory law.) Postnuptial agreements must be in writing, be signed by both spouses, and preferably carry a notary public's signature and seal.

A postmarital contract might better reflect the spouses' current reality and address areas of continuing conflict. ("Who cooks family dinner on Wednesdays?" or "Who drives the kids to weekend soccer?") The spouses may now have minor children, work full-time at independent careers, have accumulated substantial assets, and have various business interests.

Marriage happens and circumstances change. A postmarital agreement can help spouses keep pace with their lifestyles. Given the most-cited reason for divorce is conflict over finances, being proactive and addressing hot-button issues calmly and reasonably with a postmarital agreement may help the couple avoid further marital conflict.

Spouses are free to substitute their prenuptial agreement with a valid superseding agreement. One that provides more equitable terms and covers aspects of marriage that were not anticipated before the wedding.

Postmarital agreements may address a number of personal financial matters, including the following:

- Division of assets and debts in the event of divorce or legal separation;

- Provision of spousal support;

- Contribution to a child's college trust or added support beyond what the *Arizona Child Support Guidelines* mandate;

- Payment of the family's vacation and travel expenses;

- Supporting an adult family member with chronic illness or disability;

- Responsibility for domestic chores, home maintenance and repairs;

- Control of the family business;

- Inheritance as separate property despite being mingled with community assets; and

- Allocating responsibility for specific obligations during the marriage, such as utility bills or property taxes, among other things.

When separated or with divorce pending, spouses may no longer see eye-to-eye on their premarital or postmarital contract provisions. What can be done if one spouse wants the contract amended, but the other wants it revoked and gone? Or one party wants the spousal maintenance clause enforced, but not the property division clause?

These and other serious concerns could be settled during divorce negotiations and with private mediation. Before taking action that may be cause for regret later, discuss legal alternatives with an attorney.

7

Role of the Family Law Attorney

By now it should be apparent that, as beneficial as a premarital agreement can be, preparing an enforceable contract of this nature is not a weekend project for the do-it-yourselfer. Hire a lawyer for professional guidance and legal advice during the entire process, from negotiation through execution. Indeed, being represented by an attorney with substantial drafting and trial experience is the best way to ensure validity, voluntariness, and enforceability of the prenup when it matters most some 10, 20, and 30-plus years down the road.

Checklist of Attorney's Role

An attorney's involvement in the process of negotiating, interpreting, drafting, and litigating validity of a premarital agreement is not always fully understood by the client at the outset of the representation. In fact, the attorney's role may be somewhat of a mystery. Especially to a client who has little or no experience with contracts like these.

Mere mention of a premarital agreement before the wedding should raise some legitimate concerns. So long as sound legal advice is readily available and the client's questions get answered—before decisions are made and papers are signed—conversations about married life, raising a family, acquiring property, and future expectations can really do a lot of good.

What is the family law attorney's role in assisting the client with a premarital agreement? There is much to consider, including the following.

✓ Independent Counsel

An attorney can serve as "independent counsel" during prenup negotiations. Each party should have a lawyer advising him or her on marital rights and interests, along with validity requirements and any concerns about future enforceability of certain terms or conditions. This holds true for both premarital and postmarital contracts.

As discussed in *Chapter 5*, independent legal advice is a key factor in establishing voluntariness of agreement in a divorce or probate action.

✓ Experienced Litigator

An attorney's experience as a litigator applies to drafting premarital and postmarital agreements to withstand challenge. Experience matters. Having litigated voluntariness and validity in the courtroom (for or against), a competent lawyer can then advise a client on the strengths and weaknesses of the case. Starting with the client's initial position on each and every proposed provision.

✓ Community Property

An attorney can explain to the client what his or her rights to separate and community property are. And what the legal consequences will be in the event of divorce or the other spouse's death.

Arizona is among a minority of states adhering to the marital law of community property. Therefore, prenups typically include agreed provisions for succession and division of community assets and debts as was discussed in *Chapter 3*.

The decision to give up marital rights in exchange for something else, well, that is a very important individual choice to make. A choice that should only be made after discussing with the attorney, at length, what the client is being asked to surrender in exchange for what could be gained, if anything.

In order to negotiate from a position of strength and make educated decisions, the client should know the fundamentals of community property law and how it may apply to different situations.

✓ Transmutation and Commingling

An attorney can educate the client on the legal consequences of transmuting and commingling assets. The carefully drafted prenup instrument may provide for future situations where a spouse's handling of his or her separate property does not result in its being transmuted or commingled with marital property. That's despite the fact that such acts would, in absence of agreement, result in the transformation of separate assets into community assets.

Be mindful that community property is divided nearly 50/50 in divorce, while only half of the community property is included in the deceased spouse's probate estate. Take another glance at *Chapter 1* for reasons why couples choose prenuptial agreements.

✓ Spousal Maintenance

An attorney can explain the rights of a party to spousal maintenance in divorce or legal separation as compared to the outcome under specific terms in a premarital contract. There are significant tax considerations associated with the payment and receipt of spousal support, too. For example, the *Tax Cuts and Jobs Act of 2017* eliminated the alimony deduction, although there are some exceptions as mentioned previously in *Chapter 3's* discussion.

✓ Legal Costs and Fees

An attorney can discuss optional provisions arranging for payment of attorney's fees, court costs, forensic evaluator's fees, and other expert's fees. Who shall be responsible for the cost of preparing the prenuptial agreement? Who will pay costs associated with litigating validity of the prenup if challenged 5 or 15 or 30 years from now?

As noted in *Chapter 2*, if the cost of representation is beyond the reach of a party or economically dependent spouse, then the prenup may provide for payment of legal expenses by the wealthier party or spouse. Most things are negotiable.

✓ Judicial Discretion

An attorney can educate the client about the extent a prenuptial agreement may divest the judge of discretion in divorce or probate. With divorce proceedings, the judge has broad discretion in matters of spousal maintenance awards, in characterizing certain assets as community or separate property, in ordering child support in excess of what the Guidelines require, among other things. (We touched on additional support for a child in *Chapter 3* as well.)

An agreement allows the parties to determine what the outcome will be when specific conditions are met:

- How will a spouse's disability affect spousal maintenance payments?

- Who will be responsible for which marital debt?

- How will pensions and individual retirement accounts be divided?

- How much shall a parent contribute to a child's college trust, travel expenses, private lessons, or extracurricular activities?

When the equities are decided by premarital agreement, the judge has a limited discretionary role— one addressing only those matters falling outside the scope of the parties' prenup.

Just as importantly, an attorney can provide specific legal advice as to why this client might not need a marriage contract. Before advising the client on the pros and cons of a prenuptial agreement, the attorney looks to current law, shifting legal trends and recent appellate court decisions, as well as any potentially beneficial alternatives to handling business assets, large debts, inheritances, family support obligations, retirement accounts, and the like.

The attorney considers the personal information provided by the client, applies the law to that individual's situation, and then makes recommendations on how best to proceed. Every client, every marriage, and every prenup is unique.

Checklist for Initial Attorney Consultation

Before meeting with an attorney to discuss representation, gather information and documentation about personal finances and the upcoming marriage. List both general and specific questions regarding proposed premarital terms of agreement.

At the initial consultation be ready to:

✓ Discuss Circumstances

Summarize both parties' premarital circumstances. Ask what the potential benefits and detriments are of having a prenuptial agreement, given the circumstances as they are currently known. What financial disclosures are necessary?

✓ Discuss Estate Planning and Probate

Ask about estate planning alternatives to a premarital agreement. What impact will probate have? After marrying, what must be done to integrate each spouse's estate plan with the agreed conditions and terms in the parties' prenup?

✓ Discuss Alternatives

Ask the attorney to compare and contrast coverage of a premarital agreement with coverage of a negotiated separation agreement in divorce. How do they differ? How are they similar? Although settlement and divorce mediation are strongly encouraged in Arizona court proceedings, there is no guarantee the spouses' separation agreement will resolve all issues and eliminate the need for trial.

✓ Discuss Collaboration

Ask whether the attorney uses collaborative divorce techniques to assist the client in negotiating and preparing a prenuptial agreement. With a collaborative approach, each party is represented by counsel at face-to-face meetings where specific terms and conditions are discussed and negotiated. Although one attorney typically takes the lead in drafting the agreement, both lawyers assist in writing-up the papers to be signed by the parties. To foster trust and cooperation, the attorneys usually agree to refrain from representing either spouse in a later divorce or contested probate.

Before you go, there's one more thing to consider.

Premarital contracts can save on the cost of divorce litigation. How so? By eliminating the number of issues in contention. That's not hyperbole. Saving money and avoiding protracted court proceedings is possible, and likely, when the parties' prenuptial agreement specifically provides for the division of property and payment of spousal support. Of course, the agreement must be valid to be enforceable.

When a premarital contract is challenged in probate or as part of a spouse's divorce strategy, an experienced attorney is needed to successfully litigate that issue. If the judge finds the prenup is invalid, then it may be unenforceable in its entirety. The party opposing the prenup, the challenger, has the initial burden of proving the agreement is invalid. Talk to your lawyer.

Scott David Stewart, Esq.

Born and raised in Phoenix, author Scott David Stewart is the founding attorney of Stewart Law Group. His vision was to establish a unique law firm singularly focused on the clients' experiences when dealing with difficult and often intensely emotional legal matters.

With eight office locations throughout the Valley of the Sun, today this influential law firm represents clients in all matters of divorce, child custody and family law, accident and personal injury, estate planning and probate, professional license defense, DUI defense, and general criminal defense.

Early in his professional career, Scott Stewart was Deputy County Attorney in the Major Crimes Division of the Maricopa County Attorney's Office. As a felony prosecutor, Stewart honed his trial skills and developed the strategies for success that he continues to implement today in all aspects of his law practice. Since its formation, Stewart Law Group has earned the trust and respect of clients from all walks of life.

Scott Stewart is a member of the State Bar of Arizona, Maricopa County Bar Association, and American Bar Association. He has an AV Preeminent® attorney-rating from Martindale-Hubbell® and is also rated "Superb" by Avvo, Inc. Stewart Law Group is an accredited Arizona business with the Better Business Bureau having received an A+ rating.

With more than seven decades of combined legal experience, Scott Stewart and Stewart Law Group take on the most complex and challenging cases. To read more about the author, his recognitions, awards, and client testimonials, visit www.ArizonaLawGroup.com.

Stewart Law Group

777 E Thomas Rd Ste 210, Phoenix AZ 85014
Phone: 602.548.4600

Phoenix • Scottsdale • Chandler
Glendale • Mesa • Peoria
Tempe • Gilbert

www.ArizonaLawGroup.com

99514391R00046

Made in the USA
Columbia, SC
11 July 2018